T0002438

The Cost of Living Crisis

The Cost of Living Crisis (and how to get out of it)

COSTAS LAPAVITSAS

School of Oriental and African Studies and the European
Research Network on Social and Economic Policy

JAMES MEADWAY

Progressive Economy Forum

DOUG NICHOLLS

General Federation of Trade Unions

With research assistance by Matteo Giordano, School of
Oriental and African Studies and the European Research
Network on Social and Economic Policy

V

VERSO

London • New York

First published by Verso 2023
© Costas Lapavitsas, James Meadway, Doug Nicholls 2023

1 3 5 7 9 10 8 6 4 2

Verso
UK: 6 Meard Street, London W1F 0EG
US: 388 Atlantic Avenue, Brooklyn, NY 11217
versobooks.com

Verso is the imprint of New Left Books

ISBN-13: 978-1-80429-384-3
ISBN-13: 978-1-80429-386-7 (US EBK)
ISBN-13: 978-1-80429-385-0 (UK EBK)

British Library Cataloguing in Publication Data
A catalogue record for this book is available from the British Library

Library of Congress Cataloging-in-Publication Data
A catalog record for this book is available from the Library of Congress

Typeset in Sabon by Biblichor Ltd, Scotland
Printed and bound by CPI Group (UK) Ltd, Croydon CR0 4YY

Contents

Introduction

The cost-of-living crisis in the UK can be simply summed up: prices, especially of essentials, are too high, and wages, along with other working-class incomes, are too low. The basic steps to resolving the crisis are also simple: prices, especially of essentials, must be brought down, and wages, salaries, benefits, and pensions must be increased.

The big businesses that dominate production and distribution make huge profits out of high inflation, while working people lose out. It is shown in the following chapters that the source of record profits is the fall in real wages as inflation rises. To put it plainly, a large part of the income of working people is being transferred directly into the profits of big business.

The deeper roots of the cost-of-living crisis, however, lie in the profound weaknesses of the productive side of the British economy. These are apparent in the record of very low investment and poor productivity growth for many years. The productive sector in Britain has withered and performs badly, ultimately driving the cost-of-living crisis.

The plain argument that high prices, rising profits, and falling real wages go together – all having roots in weak production – is often distorted or hidden by mainstream commentary in the media and elsewhere. To explain the cost-of-living crisis it is usually argued that wages are too high, or that the government has 'printed' too much money. It is also argued that events far away, such as the war in Ukraine, are solely to blame.

The following chapters explain the reasons why these arguments are not right. The causes of the crisis are ultimately to be found in relations of property and power in the economy that have created deep problems because production is focused on the most predatory forms of profit making. It is vital that working people should avoid paying for the cost-of-living crisis, but it is even more important that the UK economy should be put on a different course to the benefit of the vast majority.

This book is the product of close collaboration between the General Federation of Trade Unions (GFTU), members of the Progressive Economics Forum (PEF), and the European Research Network on Social and Economic

Policy (EReNSEP) at the School of Oriental and African Studies, University of London (SOAS). We aimed to produce strong arguments that would place the current crisis in a historical context acting as an instrument for campaigning, a tool for education, and a launching pad for fresh solutions. Naturally, along the way, we had to bust several myths spoken daily about inflation, usually by those who benefit most from it.

Dealing with inflation must include wage increases to stop the income of workers from falling. It must also include price controls and regulation of profits to stop the transfer of income from workers to big business. More fundamentally, however, the answer must involve sustained public intervention to deal with the weaknesses of production, especially of manufacturing, aiming to rebalance the economy in favour of the productive sector. Along the same lines, Britain must become more self-reliant in the years ahead.

The route ahead for the UK ought to be the reverse of that taken over the past forty years, initiated by Margaret Thatcher. Britain's extreme unleashing of market forces involved the unprecedented privatisation and selling of public assets, wholesale deindustrialisation, and deregulation of the financial sector. It included the systematic introduction of anti-union legislation, the break-up of collective bargaining, and the erosion of the value of pensions as well as continual downward pressure on wages.

In historical terms, Britain was the first major country fully to industrialise and one of the first significantly to deindustrialise. The structure of its economy shifted drastically away from industry toward services and the City of London, and the pivot toward financial services was acute during the past four decades. Corporate economic and political power has been tremendously strengthened and, as a result, big businesses were able to help themselves to extraordinary profits. Their means of extracting profits, often with additional government funding, were shameful for an advanced country, as trade union leaders have pointed out.

The broader consequences have been disastrous as a range of major long-term weaknesses emerged, including deskilling of the labour force, low levels of investment, very weak productivity growth, persistent current account deficits, chronically low spending on infrastructure and health, education, and care, escalating inequality, entrenched imbalances between the regions of the country, and the domination of financial institutions over the lives of households.

Britain faces a historic crisis after four decades of reducing industry and manufacturing. The tremendous escalation of the cost of living, pushing entire layers of the population into destitution, is a symptom of the country's deep-seated malaise. No amount of windfall taxes, household subsidies, energy support measures and the like will deal with the deeper problems of the UK.

The present Tory Government as well as the entire political machinery of Westminster have no cure for the country's structural weaknesses. It is up to the trade unions and their social and political allies to defend what remains and argue for an industrial renaissance.

It is very encouraging that unions are rising to the challenge, but they need to work with community organisations, campaign groups, and small businesses to create a new coalition. The aim should not be simply to protest against the injustices of capitalism and defend the rights of working people. The fundamental point is that markets cannot be relied upon to pioneer advanced technology and environmental protection, nor to provide affordable food, homes, energy, transport, and utilities. Britain needs a new economic strategy to ensure the essentials of life, good jobs, and civilised conditions for all.

1

Some Definitions

In the most fundamental sense, there is nothing mysterious about how the economy operates. It is about how we work with each other to produce the things we need and use, from cars to buildings to telephones. But the way we engage in this task is organised primarily around profits, which are obtained by a small group at the top of society. Understanding how the economy works is about understanding property and power. Who owns the resources, commands the wealth produced by society, and dictates the framework of economic activity? Who creates the wealth and is obliged to accept the framework set by the resource owners?

However, this is not how economic issues, including the cost-of-living crisis, are typically presented to us. In the news and elsewhere, the economy seems like a vast and strange machine that makes demands on us or forces us and our families to take economic pain. Reports on economic affairs in the UK usually focus on the complex workings of financial markets that often seem as unpredictable as the weather, with only a few 'experts' able to understand them.

To cut through the confusion, we must first deal with some of the jargon that is normally used.

1) *Inflation* is the rate at which prices are increasing on average. If inflation is 9.4 per cent, it means that prices have gone up 9.4 per cent since this time last year. So, something which cost £10 this time last year is likely to cost £10.94 this year. The major effect of prices rising is that the value of money falls – when prices go up, you can buy less than you used to with each £1. The higher the rate of inflation, the faster your money falls in value.

It is important to remember that the inflation figure is only an average, and most goods and services will change in price faster or slower than the average figure. To find this average rise from all the different price changes, government statisticians at the Office for National Statistics (ONS) put together a 'basket of goods' which is supposed to represent what an 'average' household would consume in a month – what share of their income is spent on food, or housing, or fuel, and so on.

The average household does not really exist, of course, as people buy many different things every month. This can be a problem when dealing with inflation since people on lower earnings consistently spend proportionally more of their income on essentials like food and energy than the better off. As a result, price rises for essentials will tend to hit the poorest much harder than the inflation rate suggests.

There are two main ways for the ONS to calculate the inflation rate: the Consumer Price Index (CPI) and the Consumer Price Index with Housing costs (CPIH). CPI is the figure most often quoted by the media, since it is also the inflation figure that the Bank of England is supposed to be trying to control. The older Retail Price Index (RPI) is still sometimes cited but has not been the official measure of inflation for a decade.[1] Because all three measures involve slightly different ways of calculating the 'average' price rise, they tend to result in slightly different rates of inflation. For simplicity, we only use CPI in this book – but it is worth remembering RPI is typically higher than CPI.

The CPI is often referred to as the 'headline' rate of inflation because it is based on the standard basket of goods, including food and energy. The 'core' rate of inflation, on the other hand, excludes food and energy prices on the grounds that these prices are highly volatile and do not reflect what is going on at a deeper level.

The headline rate can contain enormous price variations that matter greatly to the standard of living of working people. In July 2022, for example, headline inflation in the UK stood at 8.8 per cent. But motor fuel prices had risen by 42.3 per cent in the previous twelve months – well above the headline figure. Clothing prices, on the other hand, rose only 6.2 per cent in the same period – so they were still rising, but at a slower rate than the headline figure.

2) *Real terms* refers to economic figures after taking account of inflation. For many decades, inflation has been consistently above zero – in other words, prices have steadily risen, but at different rates. This means that whatever £1 buys for you today, it is likely to buy less in the future, since the price of everything you could then buy with that £1 is likely to have risen by the rate of inflation.

If we want to understand the true change in someone's income, we obviously need to take account of the fact of rising prices. This is the value in 'real terms', and it is easy to work it out for changes in income – just subtract the rate of inflation from the change in income to find the change in real terms. If, for instance, a pay rise this year is 10 per cent, but inflation is 5 per cent, the real terms pay increase is 5 per cent. If the pay rise is 2 per cent, however, the real terms change in pay is a fall of 3 per cent.

In the first half of 2022 the fall in real wages in the UK was extraordinarily high by historical standards.[2] In August 2022 the main measure of inflation (the Consumer Price Index, CPI) stated that prices on average were rising by 9.6 per cent. This was the highest rate of inflation for forty years. The Office for National Statistics also estimated the change in wages and salaries over each month. Their estimate of average weekly earnings (AWE) showed that wages and salaries, excluding bonuses, rose by only 4.3 per cent in July 2022. This means that the real value of wages and salaries fell, on average, by 5.3 per cent.

3) *Supply and demand* refer to how we produce, buy, and sell goods and services by using money.

Supply refers to the amount of a good or a service available to buy at any point in time. If there is an increase in that amount, the supply of that particular good has increased. Following this simple logic, if we take all the goods and services produced in the country, we have aggregate supply. To be more precise, aggregate supply is the total amount of goods and services that producers are willing to supply at a given price level. It shows the total output of a country that is produced at that price level.

The Covid-19 pandemic, and the lockdowns imposed to deal with it, severely disrupted and reduced aggregate supply in the UK and across the world. The pandemic led to a deep disturbance in the way that goods and services are produced and sold – whether semiconductors or restaurant meals. It is very important to remember, however, that the disruption caused by Covid-19 came after ten years of persistent underlying weakness in the production of goods and services in the UK. The weakness of aggregate supply across society is the key to understanding inflation.

Demand is about how much of a good or service is wanted at any point in time and, crucially, whether those wanting the good or service have the money to pay for it. If demand goes up, it means more people are trying to buy a good or service with the money they have. Demand, in other words, must be effective and, in our society, that means being backed up by money. Crucially, a large part of demand also comes from firms which buy machinery, raw materials, energy, and various inputs from other firms.

As with aggregate supply, if we take demand (backed by money) across the whole economy, we will have aggregate demand. It is the effective demand for the entire output of a country, and specifies the amount of goods and services that would be purchased at a given price level. Aggregate demand is made up of consumer spending, investment spending by enterprises, government spending, and the spending of people in other countries on exports from our own country.

Demand and supply matter because in a market for any good or service we would usually expect the price to be set by firms competing for customers. But how individual firms do that in particular markets will depend on several factors, two of which are crucial for the cost-of-living crisis. The first is what is happening to aggregate supply and demand across the economy. The second is what the property structure of a particular industry looks like – which enterprises control supply, and how much market power they have.

If aggregate demand is boosted, we can expect people with money to try and buy many types of goods and services. We can also expect firms to meet this demand by increasing supply in their own markets but at the same time trying to raise prices since demand is generally rising and they are chasing after profits.

Much will depend on how strongly firms are able to increase aggregate supply. If aggregate supply is restricted, prices will rise consistently, that is, there will be inflation. Firms will, of course, still be making

profits. In important sectors and markets of the economy, where huge enterprises have great power over
supply – for instance, in energy – we can also expect
firms to increase prices in targeted ways to ensure
massive profits. Inflation offers endless opportunities
for speculative profit making by those who own and
control the productive resources of society. The price
is paid by the rest of us.

With these fundamental ideas – inflation, real terms,
supply and demand – clarified we have enough to deal
with the wrong arguments presented by the mainstream
commentary on inflation, and to show what is really
happening in the cost-of-living crisis and how it should
be confronted.

2

Aggregate Supply, Covid-19, and the War in Ukraine

Everyone recognises that Covid-19 was a catastrophic shock for the world economy. With new variants circulating, and lockdowns and restrictions recurring in different parts of the globe even in 2022, along with the continuing pressure on health-care systems, the pandemic will remain a source of serious difficulties for a long time yet.

If we set aside the public health aspect of Covid-19 and look only at its economic impact since early 2020, we can easily identify a crucial part of the inflationary surge that we are currently experiencing. Lockdowns and other restrictions were implemented by governments across the world from early 2020, starting with the lockdown of Wuhan in China on 21 January. At the height of the efforts to suppress the disease, some 2.5 billion people lived under some form of serious restrictions.

Such unprecedented restraints placed on so many countries across the world inevitably had a massive impact on economic activity. Aggregate supply was immediately disrupted as enterprises were forced to interrupt production and office work became impossible in millions of cases. Aggregate demand also collapsed as people were not allowed to live normally, and demand for services like airline travel, shopping in high streets, and restaurant meals, fell very sharply. Aggregate demand also fell because enterprises postponed their investment plans in the face of great uncertainty.

Responding to the collapse in demand, many enterprises rapidly cut back supply – especially of services – in many cases going bankrupt, or in others making staff redundant. Consequently, the overall contraction of aggregate supply was great, particularly in the UK, where the supply side has been weak for many years.

For these reasons, several countries – including the richest in the world – plunged into one of the worst recessions seen in history. Only extensive government support, which in the UK was provided mostly to 1.9 million enterprises, prevented even more widespread unemployment and misery. The support included increased spending to pay for workers' wages, such as the £70 billion furlough scheme in Britain. It also included subsidies, tax relief, postponement of tax obligations, and other measures. At the same time, credit was made widely available by central banks and rates of interest were reduced practically to zero to encourage spending.

Governments, in other words, gave a strong boost to aggregate demand. The impact of the intervention started to become obvious in 2021 as the restrictions and lockdowns were gradually lifted or softened. The layers of the population with higher incomes were able to accumulate savings at the peak of the restrictions as consumption was forcibly reduced. When the world started to open up again in 2021, their spending increased rapidly. The combined effect of increased private spending and high government expenditure propelled aggregate demand further forward.

It was at that point that the weakness of aggregate supply became obvious, especially in the UK. The surge in aggregate demand met a constrained supply and so, inevitably, the prices of many goods and services began to rise. A great pulse of inflation was felt around the world from the summer of 2021, with Britain among the countries at the forefront.

To start with, the constraints on aggregate supply were glaringly evident in relation to climate change and ecological disruptions to essential agricultural supplies across the world. Crop failures from extreme weather events like floods and droughts have become more frequent, with the price of coffee, for example, surging after droughts and frosts hit harvests in Brazil.[1] The exceptional heat over summer 2022 led to the Rhine drying up, hitting goods transport and prices across the continent.[2] Rising river water temperatures also restricted French nuclear electricity production, contributing to the energy crisis of today.[3]

The UK is dramatically exposed to global environmental conditions primarily as a result of the neoliberal economic policies pursued over the past four decades by successive governments. It became a net importer of natural gas in the early 2000s, and now imports 50 per cent of its total consumption.[4] Its self-sufficiency in food has dropped from domestic production meeting 75 per cent of consumption in 1990 to less than 60 per cent today.[5] As global supply shocks become more frequent, the UK's dependence on imports for essentials is a source of growing risk.

More broadly, the underlying weakness of aggregate supply in the UK is the result of trends and policies that have transformed the country during the past four decades. It reflects the loss of manufacturing industry, the resulting reliance on imports, the extraordinary scale of privatisation, and the dramatic changes in energy provision.

It also reflects the further shift of the economy toward services, affording even greater power to the financial sector, with the City of London enjoying an unprecedented freedom to transfer money capital across borders and make speculative profits. The result has been a huge imbalance in economic power and vitality between London and the south east and the rest of the country. Vast areas of Britain that used to excel in manufacturing have been mired in stagnation and poverty for decades.

There are two simple ways to show the deep and persistent weakness of aggregate supply in the UK.

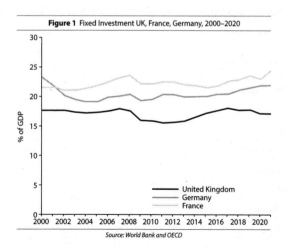

Figure 1 Fixed Investment UK, France, Germany, 2000–2020

Source: World Bank and OECD

The first is the country's very poor investment record over a long time, including particularly during the last decade. Investment is obviously the driving force of aggregate supply as enterprises renew their productive capacity and improve technology. But those who own and control productive resources in Britain have failed to invest in strengthening the country's productive structure, as is clear from Figure 1 above. During the past two decades, Britain has performed consistently worse than Germany and France, its two main European competitors. But the inadequacy of Britain's investment performance becomes even more evident in comparison with still more industrialised countries, as is shown in the following table. Indeed, the UK had the worst investment record among all the listed OECD countries. Britain's long-term investment failure is clear and of a historic order.

Fixed investment (percentage of GDP), average during 1997–2017

South Korea	30
Japan	24
France	21
United States	20
Germany	20
Italy	19
United Kingdom	16

Source: Organisation for Economic Co-operation and Development (OECD)

The second way of showing the UK's weakness is through its remarkably poor record in labour productivity.[6] The most important input into production in any country is the labour force. Aggregate supply depends ultimately on the productivity of the labour force, that is, on how efficiently and quickly workers produce the goods and services we all need. This can be measured as the amount that is produced for every hour worked. If productivity grows slowly, or even stops growing altogether, aggregate supply will not be able to respond promptly to changes in demand, and the country's productive capacity will be in trouble.

In an advanced economy, productivity will typically rise steadily every year, since enterprises are obliged to innovate by introducing new technology, and so produce more cheaply than their competitors. The real issue, however, is how fast productivity rises. If investment is sizeable and new technologies are used effectively, productivity should rise quickly, and the economy should grow rapidly. That would expand good employment, sustain rising incomes, and promote prosperity. If productivity rises slowly, however, growth stagnates, incomes fail to rise, and employment is of low quality.

It goes without saying that weak investment and weak productivity growth are closely related. If enterprises do not invest systematically, new technologies are not systematically adopted, and the labour force cannot become more productive. Even more fundamentally, though, the most important source of productivity growth in an economy is manufacturing industry. Manufacturing creates many opportunities for other economic activities to grow and expand and so improve the productivity of labour across the economy.[7] If manufacturing declines, other things being equal, productivity growth is unlikely to be strong across the economy.

The UK's record on productivity growth has been very poor for a long time, and especially during the past ten years. Figure 2 below shows how much worse the UK has performed again during the past two decades in comparison to France and Germany, its main European competitors. Bear in mind that both of these countries have also performed pretty poorly during the same period. Appalling productivity growth is the price Britain has paid for the economic policies of several decades that have favoured the service sector – especially the financial sector – at the expense of manufacturing. The apparent gains in productivity growth during the years of the credit bubble of the 2000s – with the UK seemingly closing in on productivity levels in France, Germany, and other advanced economies – were wiped out in the 2008 financial crash and the decade that

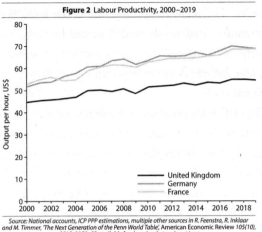

Figure 2 Labour Productivity, 2000–2019

Source: National accounts, ICP PPP estimations, multiple other sources in R. Feenstra, R. Inklaar and M. Timmer, 'The Next Generation of the Penn World Table', American Economic Review 105(10), 2015, 3150–82 available for download at ggdc.net/pwt

followed.[8] Weak productivity growth has inevitably led to a loss of competitiveness for the country in the world market. The result has been sustained problems for the UK in its international transactions.

As the country's capacity to manufacture what is necessary to meet the demands of its own people declined – and its productivity growth weakened – it was forced to import more from abroad. From being the workshop of the world in the nineteenth century, Britain became a substantial net importer of goods during the past four decades. The trade balance, showing the difference between exports (+) and imports (−) of goods, has been in persistent deficit (−) for four decades. The main reason for that is the large deficit in manufactured goods traded across borders, particularly with Europe. The contraction of manufacturing has had directly negative implications for British international trade.

The UK made good some of this trade deficit through its international transactions in services, which have generally been in surplus (+). However, since the late 1990s the surplus in services has not been enough to offset the deficit (−) in goods. The result of this overall weakness in trading in goods and services has been a persistent deficit (−) in the current account of the UK with the rest of the world, as is shown in

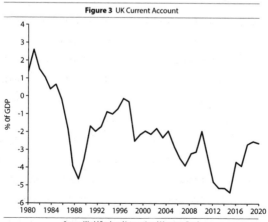

Figure 3 UK Current Account

Source: World Bank and International Monetary Fund

Figure 3. The current account is a measure of international economic transactions that includes goods, services, and other economic flows across borders, such as profit transfers, salary payments, dividends, and so on. When the overall flow is negative, the country must borrow more from abroad than it lends to the rest of the world to ensure that it can cover its current account deficit. That is, liquid capital must come into the country to make its international books balance.

And so, the UK has come to rely on regular net inflows of capital from abroad. This dependence gives enormous power to those close to financial markets to dictate terms to the UK government. The ignominious collapse of the Liz Truss Government in late 2022 ultimately came down to this factor – the financial markets were in turmoil and capital was not flowing cheaply into the UK to balance the books. Eventually the pro-finance faction of the political world got their wish, after the Bank of England threatened to withdraw its emergency funding support, and Rishi Sunak became the new prime minister of the UK.

The blow to the productive sector of the British economy over the past four decades has been of historic proportions. The country's commitment to deindustrialisation, wholesale privatisation, and global financial speculation helped create the perfect storm during the

Covid-19 pandemic, whereby we cannot even meet our own needs. Life's essentials, housing, food, and fuel, have become cruelly and unnecessarily unaffordable.

Britain has become dependent on overseas supply of goods in many crucial areas, including energy. Historically, the National Union of Mineworkers warned of the dire consequences of running down domestic energy supply and relying on privately owned, overseas providers. Agricultural workers also warned of the impact on prices and the environment that would result from the vast importation of foodstuffs.

Britain has further suffered from the unprecedented and wholesale privatisation of services and utilities. Instead of the surpluses made in particular utilities or services, for example the railways, returning to the public purse to be reinvested in service improvements, health and safety measures, and price reductions, they have been used to line the pockets of their private owners. Public wealth that could have been used to increase productive capacity was wasted to pump up company directors' bank accounts.

With the production side coming under pressure, working people, who are the most important part of production, endured a never-ending series of blows. In addition to downward pressure on wages, there has been a sustained assault on the once excellent British system of workplace pensions, where defined benefit schemes guaranteed greater certainty in retirement. The early moves to sell off social housing stock and liberalise the housing market were also a recipe for homelessness and shutting the door to independence for young people joining the labour force.

As the UK entered the pandemic, then, its economy was one in which the fundamental supports had been chewed away for many years as if by termites. The huge government intervention during the pandemic just about papered over the cracks in the structure. But as the world emerged from lockdown, the shocks that affected the globe were felt far more keenly in the creaking British economy than elsewhere.

Inflation rose sharply in the UK in 2021 primarily because aggregate supply was unable to respond to the boost in aggregate demand as private consumption rose and government expenditure increased. The true cause of the cost-of-living crisis is to be found on the side of supply, which is unable efficiently to produce what we need to live and prosper. And yet, as prices began to rise rapidly in Britain in 2021, large enterprises were able to make enormous profits at the expense of workers and the rest of society, as we will show in a later chapter.[9]

Then, in February 2022, Russia invaded Ukraine. The two countries are major suppliers of some critically important commodities. Russia is the world's largest supplier of natural gas, especially to Europe, and a huge producer of oil. Russia and Ukraine between them are the world's largest exporters of wheat, cooking oil, and a few other agricultural products. Both also have large exports of critical raw materials, including fertiliser and some rare earth minerals used especially in electronic goods.[10]

The war disrupted Ukraine's economy dramatically, affecting agricultural production and making exports far harder. Sanctions, imposed by NATO countries and their allies, in turn affected the Russian economy, restricting sales of crucial exports such as oil and gas. The result was to ratchet the prices of those key commodities greatly upwards. Natural gas prices, already rising across Europe and Asia as the lockdowns ended, skyrocketed in February and March 2022, before falling back a little later in the year. The impact of natural gas price rises has been particularly severe in Europe, where electricity supplies and, often, home heating and cooking depend on natural gas.

The result was to push inflation up still further, right across the globe. The reason is not hard to find and is rooted in the weakness of aggregate supply in the UK and elsewhere. A rise in the price of basic agricultural commodities, or industrial inputs of metals and other goods, results in a severe worsening of the terms of trade of countries that rely on importing these commodities from abroad. Simply put, it is much more expensive to bring the necessary imports into the country.

The extra cost could potentially be met by the importing country if it rapidly increased the productivity of its labour and so produced more goods that could be exported to cover the rising cost of the imports. But in the case of the UK this is not at all possible – productivity growth is non-existent at present, as we have seen.

Consequently, the additional cost of the imports has to be met by reducing profits, reducing wages, or reducing both. That is, the cost is potentially borne by enterprise owners and workers. But since the owners command much more power than the workers, the result is that prices rise to shift the cost onto workers by lowering real wages. Accelerating inflation is the means through which the increased cost of imports is borne primarily by reducing wages, while boosting profits.[11]

In sum, the structural reasons for the rise in inflation are to be found in the underlying weaknesses of aggregate supply. At the same time, opportunities were created for speculators to gamble on price movements.

By borrowing money and using it to buy up future supplies of essentials like oil, gas, and corn, speculators in financial markets can force up prices and so make additional profits from shortages. Where financial market traders, ranging from hedge funds to the trading divisions of big oil companies, are poorly regulated, the opportunities for this sort of gambling are increased. Prices have been very high, and also unstable, as a result.[12]

The point is, however, that speculation is not solely, or even primarily, to blame for the price rises, even though it has undoubtedly exacerbated some international price movements. Rather, speculation has added another unpleasant twist to the squeeze being felt by working people across the world as financiers look to exploit real instability and difficulties.

Finally, some have sought to blame Britain's exit from the European Union, completed in early 2021, as a key factor in accelerating inflation. They point to higher inflation in the UK than in the EU, with inflation excluding food and energy prices about 1.3 per cent higher than in Germany and 3 per cent higher than in France and Italy.[13]

But while the Tory Government has not handled Brexit at all well, and disruptions to trade have undoubtedly been felt in many sectors of the economy as well as having a negative impact on investment, Brexit is not the decisive factor in inflation. Eastern European EU members have seen exceptionally high inflation, with rates of 20.3 per cent in Latvia, 17.4 per cent in Czechia, and 12 per cent in Poland in 2022. Moreover, longer-standing EU members, such as Spain, currently have comparable inflation rates to the UK. Clearly Brexit cannot be blamed for this pattern.

The most important component of rising inflation in the UK is the weakness of the supply side, worsened by the profiteering of several enterprises. The problem lies primarily with the long-term weaknesses of investment and productivity failures that long pre-date Brexit.

When inflation began to accelerate in the summer and autumn of 2021, there was a widespread expectation among mainstream economists that the inflationary 'shock' would be only temporary since it resulted from the disruption of the lockdowns. Gradually it became clear that inflation was going to rise much higher than many economists expected and would remain high for a long period of time. The Bank of International Settlements, an important oversight body for the global financial system, even argued that we have now entered a new 'high inflation regime', where price rises will remain much higher than in the past.[14]

There could be no disagreement that inflation accelerated due to the shock of the pandemic, followed by the shock of the war in Ukraine. But in confronting inflation the real problem is not why it started but rather why it remains high. The fundamental reason for that is the weakness of the production side, as we have seen. However, the mainstream arguments in the media and elsewhere have been very different, and that is important because these arguments often set the terms for how inflation is dealt with by governments.

Two mainstream arguments stand out in this respect. The first claims that there is too much money in the economy generally. The second – related to the first – claims that workers (and perhaps pensioners and those on benefits) receive too much money as their income. Both are wrong and, if followed to their logical conclusions, they could take Britain down a disastrous path.

3

The Problem Is Not 'Too Much Money'

Some economists and others try to explain persistently high inflation by claiming that there is 'too much money' in the economy. They are usually known as monetarists, or supporters of the Quantity Theory of Money, who were very influential in Margaret Thatcher's governments. For working people today this view will immediately sound odd, since the problem for most of us is the exact opposite – prices are too high, and we do not have enough money. 'Too much money' would be a problem that most people would dearly love to have.

Nonetheless, for some politicians in the Conservative Party, this is the preferred explanation. Tories such as former Cabinet minister Iain Duncan Smith have blamed the Bank of England for 'printing huge sums of money' with 'quantitative easing' (QE).[1] The

BBC quoted former Tory leadership contender Tom Tugendhat as saying: 'what's triggering inflation is the lack of sound money . . . we have not been tough enough on the money supply . . . I'm afraid the quantitative easing . . . has been pumping up the economy and inflating a sugar high . . . and it's triggering this inflation.'[2] Thatcherite think-tanks, such as the Institute of Economic Affairs (IEA), make the same point.[3] They are wrong, but it is important to grasp the reasons why.

Quantitative easing is the programme implemented by the Bank of England since early 2009 to create very substantial amounts of new money electronically. Originally, this was done by the Bank in response to the global crisis of 2007–9, which hit the financial sector very hard, the idea being to support the wider economy by making sure there was plenty of money available to banks and enterprises at low interest rates. The Bank ran the programme again in 2012 and 2016, and then again, on a huge scale, as Covid-19 hit the British economy in early 2020.

The process of quantitative easing relies on many large financial institutions (especially commercial banks) holding their own accounts with the Bank of England itself, which they use as their 'reserves' – something like their own emergency savings accounts. When the Bank of England operates its QE programme, it puts more electronic money into these reserve accounts. In return, the Bank takes financial assets from those financial institutions worth the same amount.[4]

The outcome is the addition of a huge amount of newly created money into the financial system. As the UK economy sputtered during the 2010s, fresh volumes of QE money were pumped into the system by the Bank of England to try and give it a push. But it was the pandemic that really turbocharged the process. By the end of 2020, as Figure 4 shows, the total amount of new money pumped into the financial system was £895 billion, up £550 billion from the start of the

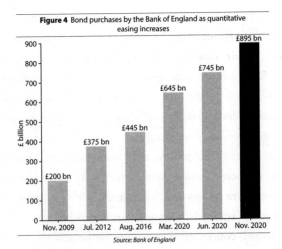

Figure 4 Bond purchases by the Bank of England as quantitative easing increases

Source: Bank of England

year. This is obviously a huge amount of money. It is, for comparison, nearly five times the entire budget of the NHS for 2021–22, and almost twenty times the defence budget for the same year. But what matters for inflation is what happens to the money.

The monetarists' idea that creating more money typically leads to inflation comes from the distant past. Milton Friedman, a leading monetarist and one of the architects of the turn to free market capitalism in the 1970s and '80s, argued that 'inflation is always and everywhere a monetary phenomenon'. He meant that if inflation was occuring, it could always be explained by changes in the amount of money in the economy.

When free market supporters today claim that QE leads to inflation, they are trying to make the same point. Their argument is that, if more money is put into the economy, then unless there is also growth in the volume of things to buy, this new money will automatically lead to price rises. There will be more money chasing the same goods and services and so (the theory goes) the people supplying the goods and services will have an incentive to raise their prices to obtain some of that extra money now circulating in the economy.

But the argument does not stand up as far as general inflation is concerned. There is no obvious link between

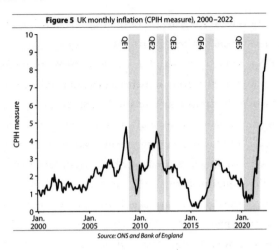

Figure 5 UK monthly inflation (CPIH measure), 2000–2022

Source: ONS and Bank of England

QE, which has been used since April 2009, and general inflation, as Figure 5 shows. Since QE started, inflation has repeatedly fallen to very low levels, even turning negative in May 2016. For significant periods of time, prices were falling, despite the new QE money in the economy.

On the other hand, QE has led to some, very specific, price increases. By creating new money and handing it to major financial institutions, the Bank of England has helped push up the price of financial and property assets. This happened because those financial institutions took the newly created money and used it to trade in financial assets (such as shares) and real estate. As a result, share prices and, especially, property prices in Britain were consistently pushed up, even as the rest of the economy suffered during Covid-19.[5]

Rising share prices and, even more, rising property prices and rents represent increases in financial wealth. So, while the supply side of the British economy was being run down and in stagnation in the 2010s, with insecure and low-paid employment becoming far more widespread, QE directly contributed to even greater wealth inequality. Perhaps the worst aspect of this, and certainly the one felt most keenly by those who entered the labour market after the financial crisis, is that by increasing wealth inequality, QE made it even harder for first-time buyers, especially in the large urban centres, to buy a home. But there was no obvious link between QE and general price inflation during the past decade.

The important point for current inflation is that during the pandemic the impact of QE shifted. The exceptional government spending in 2020, including the furlough scheme and enormous support for enterprises, was paid for to a large extent through QE. To be more precise, the government spent more and borrowed to fund that expenditure. A large part of the new debt was acquired by the Bank of England, and so a part of government spending was, in effect, financed by creating new QE money.

Some of the additional money created by QE, then, went into the productive part of the economy – for example, the £70 billion of furlough payments going directly to households.[6] But because economic activity was deliberately suppressed by lockdown, with consumer spending falling rapidly and millions kept from working, this additional government spending simply replaced lost household income and replenished business revenue. Much of it was turned into savings held by somewhat better-off households – household savings shot up to unprecedented levels over 2020 and into 2021. The ONS estimates that households saved £140 billion extra during the lockdowns.[7] These savings are now providing a cushion for many households in the face of rising prices. But they are not *causing* those prices to rise.[8]

To sum up, inflation today is not the result of more money being created. QE has been used for more than a decade in Britain with no obvious impact on inflation. When it was cranked up again during the pandemic, it acted to compensate for the dramatic collapse in demand and incomes that the lockdowns had triggered.

4

The Problem Is Not That Wages Are Too High

As we have seen, those who claim that QE and 'money printing' caused today's inflation are on shaky ground. A more common argument, however, is that a 'wage-price spiral' is either already operating or is about to kick in.

A 'wage-price spiral' is meant to describe a situation in which, because wages are rising, companies are forced to push up the prices they charge. This in turn leads to worker demands for higher wages, forcing further price rises, and so on. Inflation, so the argument goes, takes off.

This is the argument senior Tory politicians have used to deny workers in the public sector a pay rise that is equal to inflation.[1] The Governor of the Bank of England, Andrew Bailey, tried to make the same point when he said workers should exercise 'pay restraint'. In plain English, 'pay restraint' means not asking for pay rises that match inflation.

It is immediately obvious what the problem is with this argument: wages for most people in Britain are low and have been so for a long time. For a decade and a half, even though inflation has been low for much of the time, wage and salary increases were even lower. As a result, in early 2020, when Covid-19 struck, average earnings in real terms were below their level a decade earlier. Figure 6 shows what happened to real wages from 2006 to January 2020.

It is important for workers to realise how unusual this is. Except for periods of recession – which happened

Figure 6 Real Average Weekly Earnings (seasonally adjusted), 2015 £, 2006–2020

Source: ONS, Monthly Wages Survey
Note: For the Real Average Weekly Earnings, the figure is for total pay (including bonuses)

frequently but did not last long – wages in real terms rose consistently since the end of the Second World War, sometimes relatively fast and sometimes slowly. But after 2010, this steady growth in real, earned income stopped. This 'lost decade' is almost unprecedented in modern British history. Only in the early years of the Industrial Revolution, in the late eighteenth and early nineteenth century, when factories were first being built and truly grim conditions were imposed on the workers herded into them, do we find something similar.

During the 2010s, as the income of those who earned it through work declined, the income of those who derived it from wealth increased. To realise how important this is, think first of everything that is produced in the economy annually – all the goods and services produced and sold in a twelve-month period. Economists try to estimate the value of this output by using a measure called Gross Domestic Product (GDP). It is far from perfect, since it ignores important work contributions, such as housework and care work in families, but it still gives a reasonable guide to the value of output in the economy as a whole.

Since all the output is eventually sold, GDP also gives the total 'national income' out of which everyone who works in the economy, or who owns wealth, would draw their own personal income.[2] This means that the share that everyone receives is important to deciding how fair the economy is. Think of it as like slicing up a pie, with each slice going either to those who work for a living or to those who own wealth. How national income is divided tells us much about what is happening in the economy – who is doing better and who is doing worse.

Figure 7 shows what has happened to the size of the slice going to workers, and the size of the slice going to capitalists, for the past thirty years. It is quite clear that the workers' share has shrunk for the past decade. Employed workers have been receiving a smaller and smaller share of the pie since 2010, when austerity

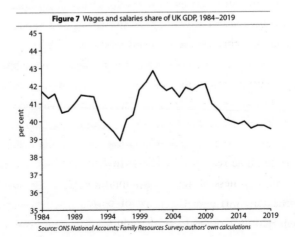

Figure 7 Wages and salaries share of UK GDP, 1984–2019

Source: ONS National Accounts; Family Resources Survey; authors' own calculations

began under the Conservative–Liberal Democrat 'Coalition' Government led by David Cameron.

Entering the pandemic in 2020, those at work in Britain were already losing out in two vital ways. First, on an individual level, most workers had seen the value of their wage or salary fall in real terms, as it had not kept pace with prices. Political pressure to ease austerity had produced some improvement by the end of the 2010s, but for most people this was not enough to compensate for the earlier decline. Second, this fall in real wages and prices was happening while workers as a whole were seeing their slice of the economic pie get smaller and smaller. To put it plainly, the class of people who own and control resources and other wealth scored a victory over the class of people who have to work to earn a living. Workers have been losing out to capitalists for a long time in the UK.

It is a very similar story if we look at the other kinds of income that most people rely on. The number of self-employed people has grown hugely in the past twenty years and reached 4 million in 2019. But average earnings for the self-employed have fallen dramatically since the crisis of 2007–9, dropping by 13 per cent in real terms from 2008 to 2019. Over half of the self-employed were earning less than £300 a week in 2019.[3]

It is notorious that benefits have been radically cut since the Cameron Government introduced austerity in 2010. On average, an out-of-work family was £1,600 worse off a year in 2021 than they would have been without the spending cuts.[4] For an out-of-work single parent things were far worse – the shortfall due to the cuts was £2,700. These huge declines in real terms were made much worse in the early 2020s.

Pensioners, meanwhile, were supposedly protected by the 'triple lock' on the state pension. This guarantees a minimum annual increase in the state pension that is equal to whatever is highest among the rate of inflation, average pay growth, or 2.5 per cent. But even if the state pension was protected, other pensioner incomes, including several benefits that pensioners rely on, were cut. The result is that the average income for pensioners has barely increased in a decade. In 2010, the average single pensioner income was £285 a week; by the end of March 2020 it had reached £298.[5]

These disastrous falls in income for workers and pensioners occurred before the pandemic. In 2020, workers' incomes were protected through the furlough scheme and other measures. However, the government's own forecasts now show that in the next few years real wages are expected to fall even further – by 7.1 per cent over the next two years, the biggest decline in living standards in Britain's modern history.[6]

Whatever it is that is driving inflation in the UK, it is not high wages. Wages have been low for a long time and are now falling very fast in real terms. There is no 'wage-price spiral' in the UK. Instead, there is a brazen attempt to secure even more profits for the owners of resources and wealth, who benefited greatly during the disaster of the past decade.

5

The Problem, Then, Is That Profits Are Too High

Sometimes economic phenomena can have very simple explanations. If prices are rising rapidly, but most people's incomes – whether wages, pensions, or benefits – are not going up so quickly, someone must be taking the difference. It is not hard to work out who that is. The difference between much higher prices and incomes failing to keep up is taken as greatly increased profits, especially by big companies.

Profits for the 350 biggest companies listed on the London stock exchange are 73 per cent higher than they were in 2019, just before the pandemic.[1] For some, like oil and gas companies, the increases in profits have been spectacular.[2] Shell and BP between them made £40 billion in profit on their global operations last year – more than twice the £19 billion increase in domestic energy prices. For reference, a person on the average 2020 UK wage would have to work 1,036,269 years to make £40 billion![3] In July 2022, British Gas announced an incredible *fivefold* increase in its half-yearly profits.[4]

It is these profit increases, not increased wages, that account for rising prices. If we add up the total amount by which prices have risen in Britain since October 2021 and compare it to the increase in profits, then the increase in profits accounts for nearly 60 per cent of the increase in prices; over the same period, the total increase in wages accounts for just 8 per cent.[5]

There is no 'wage-price spiral' in the UK. What exists is a relentless rise in profits that takes advantage of rising prices, boosting profit margins, and keeping prices high.[6]

It is important to understand what profits are to appreciate why they are such a problem for inflation today. To produce anything, a business, from the smallest to the largest, will need supplies. Typically, these will be plant and buildings in which to produce or sell goods and services; raw materials, such as water supply and electricity; and the machinery and equipment necessary for production. Above all, businesses will need to hire workers with the appropriate skills and a willingness to work. All of these are costs that must be met, or else nothing will be produced or sold. Buildings are rented, water and energy are regularly paid for, and workers receive wages.

Crucially, while wages are a necessary payment for production to happen – a cost that has to be covered, whether what is being produced are cars or calls answered in a call centre – profits are very different. They are what an enterprise can claim out of its sales revenue in addition to recouping the necessary costs of production, such as wages and raw materials. The simplest way to think about it is as a 'mark-up' on the costs of production, a regular percentage that the capitalist can add to the costs and claim as income. The bigger an enterprise can make its mark-up, the bigger will be its profits.

Profit mark-ups have been rising for some time. The Competition and Markets Authority reports that mark-ups on costs charged by the biggest and most profitable companies in Britain rose from 58 per cent in 2002 to 82 per cent by 2020, as the pandemic hit.[7] The Bank of England knows this is happening. A report in May 2022 from its 'regional agents' – who are employed by the Bank to assess economic conditions throughout the country – found that 'companies reported passing on the higher costs to consumer prices to a greater extent than normal'.[8]

Sometimes these high profits are justified by claiming that, today, it is often pension funds that own companies and therefore pensioners benefit from high profits. This is not correct. Pension funds have been selling off their shareholdings in British companies for a long time. Today only 6 per cent of the money saved in UK pension funds is invested in UK companies.[9] Just 0.2 per cent of the total value of UK pension funds is invested in BP and Shell.[10] The majority of UK pension funds invest their capital in bonds, that is, securities issued by governments and corporations that are supposed to be paid regardless of the level of profits.[11]

It has to be said, finally, that not every enterprise has benefited from high prices since 2021. Many small businesses are also at the mercy of big suppliers who are driving up prices in order to make extra profits. The problem of inflation lies with big businesses that are in a position to exploit their market power and take advantage of rising prices. They make sure that the prices that must be paid by households and smaller businesses, including the self-employed, are higher. For big businesses, rapid inflation has meant a bonanza of profits.

In light of all that, the true causes of present-day inflation in the UK are clear:

- The aggregate supply of goods and services has been weak for many years.

- The pandemic delivered a major shock to aggregate supply and caused worldwide supply disruption. The war in Ukraine greatly exacerbated the disruption of supply, especially in energy and food.
- The UK government boosted aggregate demand to confront the pandemic, mostly by supporting enterprises but also by buttressing individual incomes through furlough and other means.
- The inability of supply to respond adequately to demand led to price increases for key goods and services in the UK and across the world.
- Big companies, even in sectors where supply was seriously disturbed, took advantage of rising prices to boost their profits, greatly increasing their mark-ups.
- Growing profits are behind the persistence of inflation in 2022 and beyond, not wages that have failed to keep up with rising prices.

Inflation in the end is a matter of struggle between workers and capitalists for the distribution of the value that is produced. If aggregate demand is pushing prices up and wages are not keeping pace with the price increases, then quite simply capitalists are obtaining a larger share of the value produced in the country by having greater profits. The loss of income for workers in real terms is a direct gain for capitalists.

The extraordinary profits of big businesses in the UK and across the world in 2021–22 are not in the slightest due to technological or managerial efficiency, much less resulting from risk taking or opening up new avenues of production, as mainstream economists usually like to think. They are purely the result of an income transfer directly out of workers' wages into capitalist profits. They represent a tremendous worsening of income distribution in the UK after an already terrible decade. In short, they are a national disgrace.

This is the proper light in which to understand an argument increasingly used by Andrew Bailey, the Governor of the Bank of England, among others. This is the claim that expectations of higher future inflation can turn into higher wage demands and so fuel the 'wage-price spiral'. The Governor argued that:

> Monetary policy has to be set . . . while keeping our focus on inflation and inflation expectations . . . I would pick out the risks from domestic price and wage setting, and this explains why at the MPC's last meeting we adopted language which made clear that if we see signs of greater persistence of inflation, and price and wage setting would be such signs, we will have to act forcefully.[12]

Bailey and other mainstream economists claim that *expectations* of future inflation feed back into wage demands today, which then get turned by firms into higher prices, adding to *actual* inflation today.

But the evidence for such a causal relation between expectations about inflation and actual prices is close to non-existent. A recent paper published by the US central bank, the Federal Reserve, surveying all the evidence available, found that this belief 'rests on extremely shaky foundations'.[13] For most people, most of the time, 'expectations' about future inflation have little impact on their behaviour today. Workers are certainly not in a position easily to claim higher wages. Most businesses do not have the kind of market power that a few giant multinationals enjoy, and they are also forced to take whatever prices the market pushes onto them.

At best, most of us, if we have an expectation of higher inflation in the future, might consider buying some durable goods sooner than we planned – buying a new TV now, rather than next year, for example. But this is obviously not an option when it comes to energy to heat a home, or food, or petrol – all the things that have been rising fastest in price.

The story about managing the 'expectations' of *future* inflation is a smokescreen to persuade workers to accept the tremendous income loss and transfer to profits that is taking place *right now*. It is also the reason that the Bank of England gives for putting up interest rates. We will see in the last chapter why this will hurt most people, and workers in particular.

6

How Not to Deal with High Inflation

High inflation is a source of huge profits for big businesses, but it is also a threat to the very powerful financial interests in the UK. Finance is about debt, and the value of debt falls over time – if there is inflation of 10 per cent, then £1 loaned a year ago will now be worth around 90p of its original value. Financiers and other financial operators are worried that high inflation will disturb the mechanisms through which they lend money and make profits. Things could become even more complicated for financial interests if higher inflation in the UK weakened the pound relative to the dollar, or the euro. Financial transactions globally would be damaged, and the position of the City of London as a global financial centre would take a knock.

To prevent further increases in inflation and protect financial interests, the Bank of England, like other major central banks around the world, is now pursuing what it calls a 'tightening' of monetary policy. This means, primarily, that it is raising the interest rate it controls – the so-called 'base rate' at which the Bank lends to commercial banks – and in late 2022 it started to reverse its policy of money creation through QE.

The theory is that by increasing the 'base rate' the Bank will cause interest rates in general to rise. If interest rates go up, borrowing will become more expensive, but saving will look more attractive. Firms and households will choose to borrow less and will also spend less and save more. If there is less spending by firms and households, the thinking goes, aggregate demand will decline, and prices should begin to come down.

Except that this is not the whole story, or rather, it is a very prettified account of what is likely to happen. For, if aggregate demand falls, less will be sold, firms will have less need to employ workers, and the economy will be pushed toward recession. If a recession begins to take shape – as is already looking very likely for the end of 2022 and 2023 in the UK – workers will be even less prepared to demand higher wages as the job market tightens. Prices will fall as economic activity contracts, but businesses will also take part of the hit as less is sold, and some might be forced to close.

Controlling inflation through a recession is not something that those who make policy, or those who own resources and property, are easily willing to contemplate. A recession – particularly if it is deep – would also mean significant dangers and costs for them. What is happening, then, is a deliberate effort to create a political and economic environment that will frighten workers into accepting wage cuts.

Governor Bailey's insistence that workers exercise 'wage restraint' – that is, do not ask for wage rises that match or beat inflation – aims at precisely this result. The Bank of England's bloodcurdling forecasts of prolonged recession and unemployment contribute to the same message. As the *Financial Times* put it, the Bank of England 'wants us to feel poorer, spend less and be more fearful about demanding pay increases'.[1] And, of course, the Tory Treasury, insisting that public sector workers cannot have inflation-matching pay rises, pushes in the same direction.

If it works, it might eventually have some impact on inflation, but profits would certainly be protected. It is more likely, however, that the policy will fail, and we will end up with a recession *together* with inflation that is still high – a deadly combination that economists call 'stagflation'. The reason is simple. Cutting the real wages of teachers or call-centre workers or delivery riders in Britain does not, for instance, make the gas we import from Qatar any cheaper. Not a single extra silicon chip will be produced by refusing to pay nurses properly. Similar arguments apply to raising interest rates. There is no interest rate in London so high that it will end the war in Ukraine. The cause of the present inflation is not workers' wages, or pensions, or benefits.

Aggregate supply weakness in the UK and worldwide supply disruption is ultimately behind inflation. Squeezing aggregate demand and clobbering the living standards of working people is an incredibly inefficient way of dealing with the problem, driven by the determination to protect profits. The proper answer is to protect the income of workers, shift the burden of confronting inflation onto profits, and intervene to deal with the profound weakness of the supply side.

Government packages to help with energy bills, like the Energy Price Guarantee that somewhat 'caps' household energy bills, however welcome that support may be, will not address the systemic and power relationships that we have highlighted here.

Far worse, however, are attempts by the Tory Government of Rishi Sunak to return to austerity measures, with significant cuts to spending (and increased taxes on workers and the middle class) scheduled to start in 2024. It is, of course, a measure of the government's political weakness that an immediate return to the austerity policy of the 2010s has not been possible. But even this slight deferral represents a return to the disastrous policies that left the UK and its population so exposed to the global inflationary shocks of the early 2020s. Austerity policies undermined public services and public investment, cut wages, salaries and working-class incomes, and privileged profits above productive investment. If austerity policies are implemented as Sunak's government intends, the UK's fundamental economic problems will become much worse.

7

For a Real Plan to Tackle Inflation: Three Main Pillars

The policies that we need to deal with inflation should aim to protect the interests of the majority. They must not be driven by a relentless effort to protect profits, creating terrible problems for society, as was shown in the previous chapters. The UK needs socially minded policies that will have the interests of workers, the poor, and the self-employed at the forefront. Such policies must be based on three pillars.

First, wage rises should be at least equal to the rate of inflation across the board. There must be no more income losses and certainly no income transfers from workers to capitalists. But this is only the first step. Wage rises should in truth be above the rate of inflation, to begin to claw back some of the extraordinary losses that workers in the UK have had to endure over the past decade and more.

There is no reason why the very large, typically very profitable companies that account for 40 per cent of all employment in the UK should not be making pay rises that at least match the rate of inflation.[1] There is also no reason why public sector workers should not be receiving pay increases that are at least equal to inflation, when the government was able to spend enormous amounts of money to protect enterprises in 2020–21. The key to winning these increases lies with union organisation and collective bargaining. Industrial disputes are already picking up very rapidly, but we need unions to be active and to emerge in many more sectors.[2]

Above all, we need collective bargaining across the economy. Inevitably this will mean sustained state intervention, as new labour laws are urgently needed. The main target of anti-worker and anti-trade-union legislation for more than four decades has been to break up collective bargaining. The legislation has also tried to make effective industrial and strike action as difficult as possible, and to outlaw solidarity action between different groups of workers. In 1980, more than 80 per cent of the labour force received wages that were determined through some form of organised collective bargaining. Now it is less than 20 per cent.[3] It is imperative to reverse this trend.

Second, to control inflation immediately it would be necessary to restrain big business profits. There is no way this would happen through persuasion, incentives, or cajoling the property owners. Enterprises will continue to raise their mark-ups as long as they are allowed to do so. The answer lies with regulation of the pricing and operations of key sectors of the economy, for example through taxation and price controls. The aim should be to squeeze suppliers' profits rather than households' real incomes, and thus bring prices under control.

For smaller businesses, on the other hand, which are also burdened by the higher costs imposed on them by the major companies, taxation could be used to help mitigate the pressure. There is a good case for reductions in the taxes smaller employers face for employing workers, typically National Insurance contributions. It would be politically wise for the workers' movement to look for allies among small businesses that are also feeling the squeeze of the inflation surge.

Domestic gas prices in the UK offer a classic example of such policies. The price of gas across the world, but especially in Europe, surged in 2022. The UK had a weak form of price control, introduced in 2018, which in April 2022 resulted in a shocking 56 per cent increase in household gas bills. Political pressure over the summer, notably including a growing campaign to refuse to pay energy bills, led to the government introducing a very expensive but only partially effective price control for households, the Energy Price Guarantee. Using a price control effectively would mean restricting the painful surges in domestic prices, freezing the price for essential household consumption, and squeezing the outrageous profits of the major oil and gas suppliers, such as BP and Shell, to cover the cost of intervention. Other countries either have, or are looking at, more effective versions of energy price controls, such as the proposals of Germany's energy price commission.[4]

More broadly, the energy system in the UK is privatised, and this helps account in part for the high prices and poor service that have befallen us. Bringing energy retailers back into public ownership would be a simple means to begin to deal with the problem. But the real profits in the energy system are being made at the other end of the pipe, by the companies pumping the fossil fuels out of the ground. It has been estimated that an 'excess profits tax' on North Sea profits would bring in £13 billion a year for government.[5]

Elsewhere across the world, the majority of oil and gas resources are state-owned, but a policy to bring oil and gas production under public ownership in the UK would need to be considered very carefully. It may not be desirable to bring assets that face rundown and closure in the near future into public ownership. Past experience with banks has shown how public ownership has been used to dump losses on the public while allowing profits to remain in private hands. If there is a case for public ownership of gas and oil production, therefore, it needs to be made with that in mind. On the other hand, a publicly owned generator of renewable energy would be an essential component of a sound plan for energy in the future.

Third, and far more deeply and radically, confronting inflation is ultimately about dealing with the persistent malaise of aggregate supply that lies at its root. Britain needs a thorough rebalancing of its economy in favour of socially useful work rather than financial services. A coherent industrial policy is needed for that, which will rely on a restructuring of political power in the country, assigning far more responsibility to the regions compared to London.

Such an industrial policy will have to be based on a wave of public investment to renew the country's infrastructure as well as public ownership of key resources, including energy, transport, water, and more. It would also have to engage seriously with the energy transition and the catastrophic impact on the environment of unbridled capitalism in recent decades. Reliance on fossil fuels exposes this country, like all others, to the risk of international supply disruptions, and potentially higher prices in the future as reserves are depleted and more costly sources of fuel are brought into use. The International Energy Authority forecasts a 58 per cent rise in the price of natural gas by 2030, for example, but renewables costs have plummeted in recent years as technological improvements have come on-stream.[6] Likewise, improvements in energy efficiency, especially for domestic use where Britain suffers from poorly insulated homes, would rapidly save on energy use.

Looking ahead, with global harvests severely disrupted in 2022 and future forecasts also looking bleak as climate change bites, there is a need for industrial policy to develop a secure, sustainable food system for the country, breaking the UK's chronic dependency on superexploited labour (typically coming from abroad) and imported food.[7] The essential elements of modern life – notably food, energy, and transport – cannot be left to market forces and the profit motive alone. If they are, future disruptions will be translated into shortages combined with extraordinary profits for the companies that dominate production.

None of this would be possible without profound change in the financial system, with public banking being properly reintroduced and public guidance over the direction of capital investment, including the use of selective taxation and credit guidance alongside government borrowing for investment. It is also time for the UK seriously to consider broader controls over the movement of capital across borders and the resulting instability of exchange rates. In the same spirit, finally, the management of the Bank of England should be brought firmly under democratic control with full accountability of its policies. The Bank relies on public credit and it should use it to support the restructuring of the British economy in a productive direction instead of mobilising it largely to protect private banks. At the very least it would need a fuller mandate to include support for the restructuring of the British economy, a far broader selection field for its Monetary Policy Committee, and full transparency in its decision making.

Above all, what is needed is a profound shift in the balance of power at the workplace in favour of labour. In the end, the most precious productive resource that the UK has is its people. Their rights and standard of living have to be protected and improved, their energies and collective strength must be mobilised, and their communal spirit must be rejuvenated, if the country is to get out of the terrible mess that it finds itself in.

Notes

Notes

1 Some Definitions

1. RPI lost its National Statistic status in 2013.
2. Real wages fell by around 3 per cent year-on-year to June 2022 (see Office for National Statistics, 'Average weekly earnings in Great Britain, August 2022', 16 August 2022).

2 Aggregate Supply, Covid-19, and the War in Ukraine

1. 'Coffee could get even pricier as Brazil's harvest falters', *Wall Street Journal*, 21 August 2022.
2. 'Rhine waters fall again in Germany, river shipping costs rise', *Reuters*, 10 August 2022.
3. Julia Kollewe, 'EDF cuts output at nuclear power plants as French rivers get too warm', *Guardian*, 3 August 2022.
4. Department for Business, Energy and Industrial Strategy, 'Digest of UK energy statistics 2022', 28 July 2022, chapter 4.

5. Department of the Environment, Food and Rural Affairs, 'Food statistics in your pocket', 15 November 2022.

6. The two main measures of productivity are the 'output per hour worked', to measure labour productivity, and the 'Multi Factor Productivity' (MFP), which measures the changes in output unexplained by the changes in labour and capital inputs (adjusted by quality proxies).

7. See, for this argument, Rebuild Britain, *Rebuild British Manufacturing: A Strategy for Revival*, 2022.

8. See, for example, the figures given by the Office for National Statistics, 'International comparisons of UK productivity, final estimates: 2020', 20 January 2022.

9. Lord Hendy QC put the point very clearly: 'the price of these commodities does not reflect the actual cost of supply (which has not increased), it reflects that cost plus the maximum amount of profit which the producers can extract'. Institute of Employment Relations, 'The government's response to the cost-of-living crisis is nothing short of class war', 24 August 2022.

10. For example: 'Together, Russia and Ukraine account for almost 30 per cent of total global exports of wheat, nearly 20 per cent of global exports of corn (maize) and close to 80 per cent of sunflower seed products, including oils. The war has largely shut off grain exports from Ukraine and is affecting Ukrainian farmers' ability to plant the 2022 crop . . . Global food and fertiliser prices were near record highs even before Russia

invaded Ukraine in February 2022.' Daniel Maxwell, 'War in Ukraine is pushing global acute hunger to the highest level in this century', *Conversation*, 27 April 2022.

11. The main elements of this argument were developed by R. Rowthorn, 'Conflict, Inflation and Money', *Cambridge Journal of Economics* 1(3), 1977, 215–39.

12. Antonia Juhasz, 'Why are gas prices so high? These obscure traders are partly to blame', *Guardian*, 28 April 2022; Rupert Russell, 'Wall St is mostly to blame for rising commodity prices', *Jacobin*, 12 August 2022.

13. Adam S. Posen and Lucas Rengifo-Keller, 'Brexit is driving inflation higher in the UK than its European peers after identical supply shocks', Petersen Institute for International Economics, 24 May 2022.

14. See the Bank for International Settlements, *Annual Report 2022*, June 2022, at bis.org.

3 The Problem Is Not 'Too Much Money'

1. See George Grylls, 'Sunak "fuelled inflation by printing huge sums of money during pandemic"', *The Times*, 18 July 2022.

2. BBC Radio 4 Today Programme, Tory Leadership Debate July 2022.

3. The IEA offers several publications and posts linking inflation and QE, for example George Maher, 'Lessons from Ancient Rome about the perils of quantitative easing', 28 September 2021, available at iea.org.uk.

4. In simple terms, the Bank of England buys bonds (mostly public but also private) from banks and beefs up the accounts they hold with it.

5. The House of Lords Economic Affairs Select Committee, summarising the evidence on QE and inequality, said that 'On balance, the committee found that QE is likely to have exacerbated wealth inequalities in the UK. It said this was because QE's main effects act to increase the prices of assets, which primarily benefit wealthier households.' House of Lords Economic Affairs Select Committee, 'Quantitative Easing', 11 November 2021.

6. The reliance of UK governments on private finance, thereby elevating its power and control over the economy, is increasingly challenged within the Labour movement; see the Rebuild Britain pamphlet, *Government Spending and Debt: A New Approach*, 2022.

7. See the calculations in Office for National Statistics, 'Economic modelling for forced saving during the coronavirus (COVID-19) pandemic', 6 June 2022.

8. In fact, it was calculated that even the support provided by the government to households failed to compensate for the net real losses caused by rising inflation and specifically by rising energy prices. See the calculations in 'Is Cost of Living Support Enough?', jpit.uk, 2022.

4 The Problem Is Not That Wages Are Too High

1. For example, Boris Johnson speaking at the G7 meeting in Bavaria, or the Tory leadership debates. See Public and Commercial Services Union, 'Public sector pay: Tory hopefuls show contempt for workers', 18 July 2022.

2. There are some exceptions to this, if we think about those who draw their earnings from abroad. But this is a very small part of the total in the UK and can be ignored here.

3. Figures are for 'solo' self-employed (i.e. those employing no other workers). Taken from Giulia Giupponi and Xiaowei Xu, 'What does the rise of self-employment tell us about the UK labour market?', Institute of Fiscal Studies, 2020.

4. Sarah Arnold, Dominic Craddic, and Lukasz Krebel, 'How our benefits system was hollowed out over 10 years', New Economics Foundation, 20 February 2021.

5. These are the median figures for a single pensioner, before housing costs have been deducted. See Department for Work and Pensions, 'Pensioners' Incomes Series: financial year 2019 to 2020', 25 March 2021, Table 4.3.

6. Gurpree Narwan, 'Household disposable incomes are heading for their biggest fall on record', Sky News, 17 November 2022.

5 The Problem, Then, Is That Profits Are Too High

1. Unite the Union, *Unite Investigates: Corporate Profiteering and the Cost of Living Crisis*, June 2022.

2. As was argued powerfully by Lord John Hendy QC, in 'A transfer of wealth from labour to capital unparalleled since the 1930s', *Morning Star*, n.d.

3. The average gross salary across the UK in 2020 was estimated by the ONS at £38,600 for full-time employees. See Office for National Statistics, 'Annual Survey of Hours and Earnings (ASHE) – estimates of annual earnings for the UK, England, England excluding London, and the regions, for the 90 to 99 percentiles: 2019 to 2020', 9 July 2021.

4. See the reports in Noor Nanji, 'British Gas owner Centrica and Shell see profits soar as bills rise', BBC, 28 July 2022.

5. These figures are from the report by Unite the Union, *Unite Investigates: Corporate Profiteering and the Cost of Living Crisis*, June 2022. Unite looked at the Office for National Statistics aggregate figures for 'Gross Operating Surplus' (meaning profits) and found that they account for 58.7 per cent of the increase in the amounts paid for goods and services since October 2021. The increase in 'unit labour cost' (meaning wage and salary costs, plus any additional benefits paid by employers) accounted for only 8.3 per cent.

6. It is a similar story across the developed world. From mid-2020 to the end of 2021, covering the pandemic, 53.9 per cent of price rises in the US were driven by increased corporate profits. Only 7.9 per cent of the price rises could be attributed to increasing labour costs, well below the average 61.8 per cent average for 1979–2019. The remainder was due to a

combination of non-labour costs like raw materials, energy, or machinery. Figures at Adam Tooze, 'Chartbook #122: What drives inflation?', *Chartbook*, 17 May 2022.

7. See: Competition and Markets Authority, 'The State of UK Competition', April 2022, p. 96 available at assets.publishing. service.gov.uk.

8. Bank of England, *Monetary Policy Report*, May 2022.

9. Mercer, *European Asset Allocation Survey*, 2019, Chart 5, info.mercer.com.

10. Philip Inman, 'Windfall tax on oil giants won't hurt British pensioners, thinktank finds', *Observer*, 8 May 2022.

11. Mercer, *European Asset Allocation Survey*, 2019, Chart 5, info.mercer.com.

12. Andrew Bailey, Mansion House speech, 19 July 2022.

13. Jeremy B. Rudd, 'Why do we think that inflation expectations matter for inflation? (And should we?)', *Finance and Economics Discussion Series 2021-062*, Washington: Board of Governors of the Federal Reserve System.

6 How Not to Deal with High Inflation

1. Chris Giles, 'The Bank of England should make it clear when it gives us a kicking', *Financial Times*, 11 May 2022.

7 For a Real Plan to Tackle Inflation: Three Main Pillars

1. Figures for employment in firms employing 250 or more people. From Department for Business, Energy and Industrial Strategy,

'Business population estimates for the UK and regions 2021: statistical release', 7 October 2021.

2. Tom Wall, 'Industrial disputes in UK at highest in five years as inflation hits pay', *Observer*, 2 April 2022.

3. The Institute of Employment Rights (IER) has mapped the history of this decline and its impact and proposed a comprehensive manifesto for the reintroduction of positive labour law and collective bargaining. See the IER resources available at ier.org.uk/resources.

4. 'Germany finalises details of planned gas price cap', *Reuters*, 31 October 2022.

5. Figures from the Tax Justice UK blog: 'A North Sea excess profits tax could turn the tide of the cost of living crisis', taxjustice.uk, 25 May 2022.

6. 'Natural gas price forecasts: 2021, 2022 and long term to 2050', knoema.com, 29 May 2022.

7. Cecilia Nowell, 'Waterlogged wheat, rotting oranges: five crops devastated by a year of extreme weather', *Guardian*, 1 November 2022.